Glass Painting
made easy

Glass Painting
made easy

Series Editors: Susan & Martin Penny

David & Charles

A DAVID & CHARLES BOOK

First published in hardback the UK in 1998
Reprinted 1998, 1999, 2000
First published in paperback in the UK 2003

Distributed in North America
by F&W Publications, Inc.
4700 E. Galbraith Rd.
Cincinnati, OH 45236
1-800-289-0963

A catalogue record for this book is available from the British Library.

ISBN 0 7153 1503 X (paperback)

Series Editors: Susan & Martin Penny • Designed by Penny & Penny • Illustrations: Fred Fieber at Red Crayola
Photography: Ashton James; Jon Stone • Stylist: Susan Penny

Printed in Italy by Stige SpA
for David & Charles
Brunel House Newton Abbot Devon

David & Charles books are available from all good bookshops.
In case of difficulty, write to us at David & Charles *Direct*, PO Box 6, Newton Abbot,
TQ12 2DW quoting reference M001, or call our credit card hotline on 01626 334555.

Visit our website at www.davidandcharles.co.uk

Contents

Introduction to Glass Painting

Glass Painting Made Easy is a complete guide to the craft of glass painting; to produce beautifully painted glassware you must first learn a little about the paint, and how it will react on the surface of the glass. By following the step-by-step instructions, you will quickly learn the mysteries of this age-old craft technique

Essential equipment

Below is a list of the essential equipment needed to paint on glass:

- **Paper** – use copier paper to make a tracing of the design.
- **Typewriter carbon paper** – use for transferring a design to the glass.
- **Artist's paintbrush** - used to apply glass paint to the surface of the glass.
- **Stencil brush** - used with a stencil for applying paint to the glass.
- **Decorator's paintbrush** – used for flogging the paint surface.
- **Paint dish** – flat plastic microwave dish or fresh food tray.
- **Kitchen paper** – for mopping up spills.
- **Cotton buds** – used to make patterns in wet glass paint.
- **Soft sponge** – used to make a mottled surface on wet glass paint.
- **Masking tape** – used to mask off areas of glass that you do not want to paint
- **Thick plastic sheet** – used as a base for making shapes with gel.
- **Petroleum jelly** – used for coating the plastic sheet before spreading the gel.
- **Superglue** – used to attach jewels to the surface of the glass.
- **Hair dryer** – useful for drying paint between colour changes.
- **Cutting knife** – craft knife, sharp enough to remove dried glass paint.
- **Oven** – used for hardening porcelain paint.

Tips for special effects

- ✔ Attach jewellery stones with superglue
- ✔ Make shapes from gel, then attach to the surface of the project
- ✔ Use a wide brush to create a 'dragged' effect in the paint

- ✔ Draw shapes in the wet glass paint using a blunt-ended tool
- ✔ Use a sponge to create a 'mottled' effect on the surface of the paint
- ✔ Mix paint colours together in swirls on the surface of the glass
- ✔ Use a flat-ended brush to flog the surface of the paint giving it a furry effect

Tips for preparing the glass

- ✔ Wash in hot soapy water, before you start
- ✔ Dry thoroughly, then wipe the surface with white spirit to remove any grease
- ✔ Leave washed glass to cool before painting

Tips for painting on glass

✔ Lay the glass flat on a pad of kitchen paper
✔ Do not work with a large area of wet paint
✔ Use water-based paint in a warm, dry room

✔ Spread the paint evenly over the glass
✔ Use solvent paint, in a well ventilated room
✔ Do not rush the painting, allow plenty of drying time between colours
✔ Clean equipment and brushes regularly

Design inspiration

✔ Use a photocopier to reduce or enlarge a design to fit the glass
✔ Old gardening and wildlife magazines are a good source of design inspiration
✔ Simple shapes make the best designs
✔ Try out different colour combinations on an old jam jar
✔ Check out junk shops for interesting glass

Caring for decorated glass

✔ Wash glass carefully in warm soapy water, dry with a soft cloth, then buff to a shine
✔ Colourless varnish will help protect the surface, but will dull the paint
✔ Porcelain paint wears better than glass paint
✔ Decorated glass is not dishwasher safe

Choosing the right paint

To help you understand a little more about the paint you will be working with, listed below are some of the plus and minus points for each paint.

● **Glass paint** – Water-based
 Very easy to use
 Brushes can be washed in water
 Completely dry in about two days
 Mistakes can be removed with a knife
 Can be washed in warm soapy water
 Not dishwasher safe
● **Glass paint** – Solvent-based
 Strong smell
 Work in a well ventilated room
 Brushes must be cleaned in white spirit
 Brush marks difficult to remove
 Use a thinner to thin the paint
 Can be washed in warm soapy water
 Not dishwasher safe
● **Porcelain paint** – Water-based
 Needs to be thermohardened in an oven
 Baking time 35 minutes
 Gas mark 2/3, 300/325°F (150/170°C)
 Air bubbles can form on the paint surface
 Can be washed in warm soapy water
 Will wear better than glass paint
 Not dishwasher safe
● **Outliner paste**
 Easy to use, squeeze like an icing tube
 Completely dry in about two days
 Affected by temperature and humidity
 Warm, dry conditions are best
 Mistakes easily removed with a knife
● **Acrylic and Emulsion**– Water-based
 Dries patchy, needs two or three coats
 Brushes can be washed in water
● **Glitter glue**
 A mixture of glue and glitter
 Best used on a matt painted glass
 Sold in a pen-like container with a nozzle
 Can be used straight from the tube
● **Colourless varnish** – Water-based
 Wash brushes in water
 Milky solution dries to a clear finish
 Will dull glass paint colours
 Paint over outliner paste to protect it

Transferring the Design

There are many methods of transferring a design on to the surface of the glass. Which you choose depends on the style, colour and surface texture of your container. The recommended method for each project is given in the instructions, but as you experiment you may prefer to use an alternative technique

Using a tracing

Trace off the design. If working on a flat piece of glass, attach the tracing to the reverse side of the glass. For curved glass, it may be necessary to cut the tracing into small sections, attaching each individually.

If the tracing does not sit flush against the glass, pack the inside with crumpled tissue paper. Follow the design lines carefully with a water-proof drawing pen or outliner paste.

Using carbon paper

To transfer the design to mirror glass, place typewriter carbon paper between the glass and the tracing. Draw over the lines firmly using a ball-point pen. Carefully remove the tracing and the carbon paper from the glass.

To transfer the design to a multi-sided object, wrap carbon paper then the tracing around the container; or cut the tracing into pieces, working each side separately.

Using a stencil

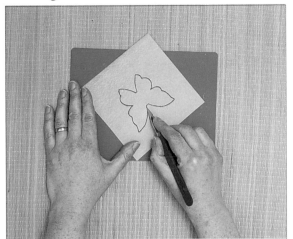

To make a stencil, place typewriter carbon paper between stencil card and the design tracing, draw over the lines. Using a sharp knife, cut the stencil card starting from the centre – this will ensure the structure stays firm. Move the stencil around as you cut, drawing the knife towards you. Use the stencil to paint the glass or as a guide for the outliner paste (see below).

If you are worried about keeping your hand steady when using outliner, then use the inside edge of a stencil as a guide. Make a stencil of the design then attach to the glass. Draw around the inside edge of the stencil using outliner paste. Allow to dry before removing the stencil.

Working freehand

You will need to use this method if you are working on frosted glass, where a tracing will not show through; or on dark coloured glass where the carbon paper transfer lines will be lost. Using a soft pencil or a chinagraph pencil, draw the design lines freehand on to the surface of the glass. Paint over the pencil lines with light coloured outliner paste.

There is a simple way to draw level lines freehand around a cylindrical container. Fill the container with water to the point where you want the lowest line to be. Turn the container slowly while marking a line on the surface of the glass. To draw higher lines, add more water.

Painting Techniques

Paint can be applied to glass using a number of different methods: outliner, gel and glitter glue can be used straight from the tube; while glass, porcelain, acrylic and emulsion paint needs to be painted on with a brush. Use a cotton bud, the end of a brush, or a sponge to add a decorative finish to the surface

Using outliner paste

Squeeze the tube of outliner gently, keeping your hand steady, as if using an icing tube. The spread of the paste depends on the room temperature: warm dry conditions are best.

Using porcelain paint

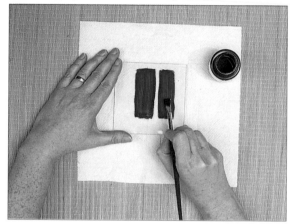

Porcelain paint will wear better than glass paint; after painting, leave for 24 hours, then bake in a domestic oven for 35 minutes at gas mark 2/3, 300/325°F (150/170°C).

Using glass paint

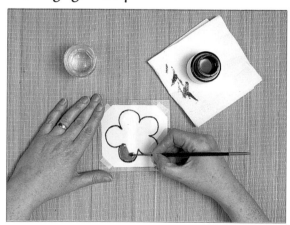

Use a paintbrush to spread water or solvent-based glass paint evenly on to the surface of the glass. Colours can be mixed together in a dish or on the glass.

Using acrylic paint

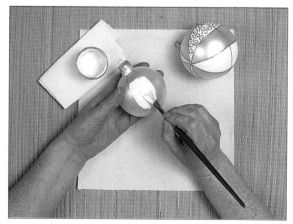

Both acrylic and emulsion paint can be used on glass. As the paint dries it will shrink, leaving some areas of the glass showing. Use a second or third coat for complete coverage.

Using gel

Water-based gel can be applied directly from the tube on to the surface of clean glass and then spread with a knife; or stir the gel rapidly and it will become liquid and can be applied with a brush. Drying time depends of the thickness of the gel, but it should be tacky in about an hour, fully dry in a week; some shrinkage will occur whilst drying. Use water to clean spills and equipment.

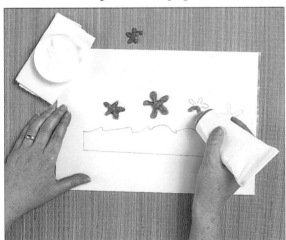

Water-based gel can be used to make three-dimensional shapes. Place the design under a sheet of thick plastic, coated with petroleum jelly, then squeeze the gel within the design lines. When dry, the gel will have shrunk away from the plastic, and can be glued on to the surface of the project.

Using glitter glue

Glitter glue is a mixture of paper glue and glitter, sold in a pen-like container with a nozzle. The glue can be gently squeezed directly on to the surface of the glass. After use, wipe the nozzle with kitchen paper and replace the cap. Glitter glue works best on glass that has been coated with matt paint.

Using varnish

Matt or gloss varnish can be used to protect painted glass. Although the milky-looking varnish will dry to a clear finish, it will still dull the paint colours, making them far less luminous. Carefully, paint over the outliner, using a fine paintbrush, which will protect it, without affecting the finish.

Making a pattern

Paint the surface of the glass with one or two glass paint colours, use a brush to mix the colours together. While the paint is still wet, use a cotton bud or a fine artist's paintbrush to draw swirls in the paint. Replace the cotton bud; or wash the paintbrush regularly in clean water.

Pouncing through a stencil

Place the stencil over the glass, holding in place with masking tape. Load a small flat-ended stencil brush with glass paint, then pounce the brush on to kitchen paper to remove the excess paint. Pounce the almost dry brush on to the surface of the glass, within the cut areas of the stencil.

Sponging on glass

Use masking tape to mask off the areas of the glass that you do not want to be sponged. Pick up some glass paint on to a small piece of kitchen sponge, then dab on to the tumbler in the areas not covered by the masking tape. Build up the paint until the glass between the tape is covered.

Flogging the paint surface

Add blobs of paint to a wet, painted surface. Holding a flat ended paintbrush in the palm of your hand, lightly flog the surface of the glass paint: this is done by tapping the paint with the ends of the bristles lightly, to give a furry effect to the paint while merging the colours together.

Hints and Tips

When working on a large area of wet glass paint, great care should be taken to avoid smudging the paint. Here you will find useful advise for drying the paint quickly, and for removing mistakes if your paintbrush slips, plus tip for washing and caring for you glassware

Removing mistakes

If you make a mistake while using glass paint or outliner paste: leave to dry, then use a sharp craft knife to carefully scrape away the dry paint before re-painting.

Quick drying

If you are working on a very complex design and need to dry the paint between colour changes: use a hair dryer on the lowest heat setting to touch dry the paint.

Attaching jewels

Use super glue to attach jewellery stones to the surface of the glass. Draw around the stones using outliner, filling the gap between the stone and the glass.

Washing painted glass

Wash decorated glassware carefully in warm soapy water. Use a soft cloth to dry the glass, then buff to a shine. Decorated glass is not dishwasher safe.

Butterfly Jug and Tumblers

For serving water, nothing looks better than clear glass. New jugs
are cheap to buy or try your local junk shop for second-hand.
Search out old tumblers too and give them a new lease of life for
summer entertaining outdoors with these beautiful butterfly designs

Any straight-sided glass can be used to
complete this project. If you are using old
glass, check thoroughly for flaws: do not use if
it is scratched or chipped. Air bubbles within
the glass will not affect the design.
NOTE decorated glass should be washed
carefully in warm soapy water: it is not
dishwasher safe.

You will need

- Straight-sided glass jug
- Straight-sided tumbler
- Water-based glass paint – golden yellow, lemon,
  deep blue, dark blue, oriental green, prairie green
- Water-based glass paint – colourless
- Outliner paste – gold
- White paper, soft pencil, masking tape
- Kitchen paper, cocktail stick, cotton bud
- Small paintbrush
- Scissors

Transferring the motifs

1 Wash the glassware thoroughly in a bowl
of warm soapy water. Leave to dry, then
polish inside and out with a soft cloth. Hold
the jug and tumbler up to the light to check
that they are completely free of marks. Do not
start painting until they are quite dry.

2 Lay white paper over the butterfly design
motifs on page 17. Trace the designs
carefully using a soft pencil. You can use a
photocopier if you would prefer not to mark
your book or if you need to enlarge or reduce
the size of the motifs to fit your jug.

3 Cut out the butterfly motifs from the
white paper – the jug and tumbler
pictured here require two large, three medium
and three small. If you would like some of the
smaller butterflies to face in the opposite
direction, flip the tracing then re-mark the
design on the reverse side of the paper.

4 Fix the motifs to the inside of the jug,
facing outwards, using small pieces of
masking tape. If the design does not sit
flush against the glass, pack the inside of
the jug with crumpled tissue paper. If the
tracing is still not lying flat against the glass,
you may need to use another method of
transferring the motifs (see Transferring the
Design, page 9).

5 The butterflies on this jug have been painted in blue, green and yellow with a gold outline. If you would prefer to use other colours – perhaps to match your table linen, then photocopy the butterfly design motifs and use coloured pencils to try out some different colour schemes.

Adding the outliner

1 Paint the jug lying on its side on a pad made from a tea-towel, soft cloth or kitchen paper.

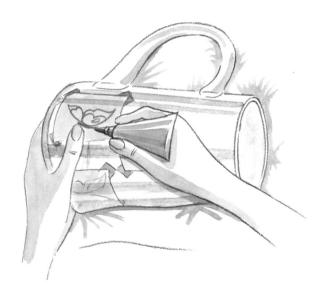

2 You will be working straight on to the glass with gold outliner, so it is important to practise on an old jar before you begin. The spread of the outliner depends on the temperature and humidity of the room: warm, dry conditions are best. If left unchecked metallic paint has a tendency to spread across the glass. Squeeze the tube gently keeping your hand steady, as if using an icing tube. Always keep kitchen roll to hand and whenever you stop, wipe the nozzle and replace the cap. Don't worry too much about a wobbly outline, as once the glass is painted, you will be looking at the colour rather than the outline. Work one motif at a time, leaving to dry

thoroughly before moving to the next. You can use a hair dryer to speed the drying process (see Hints and Tips, page 13).

3 Fortunately smudged or badly drawn lines are easily removed. You can either wipe away the excess outliner while still wet or wait until it is dry and remove it with a craft knife or the end of a cocktail stick (see Hints and Tips, page 13).

Painting the jug

1 Using a small clean paintbrush start filling in the areas to be painted. Always work with the glass flat and on one small area at a time, leaving the paint to dry thoroughly before turning the jug to the next motif – this way you will have less chance of smudging your work. Each part of the butterfly's wings should be painted by mixing two shades of the same colour. This can be done directly on to the glass. Load the brush with the lighter coloured of the two paints to be used in that area. Apply the paint generously, working quickly across the area to be filled. Lift the jug up to the light to check that the colour is even. When flat on the table the paint will look dense and uneven patches will be difficult to see.

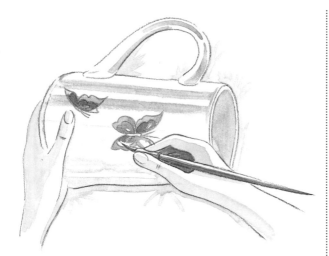

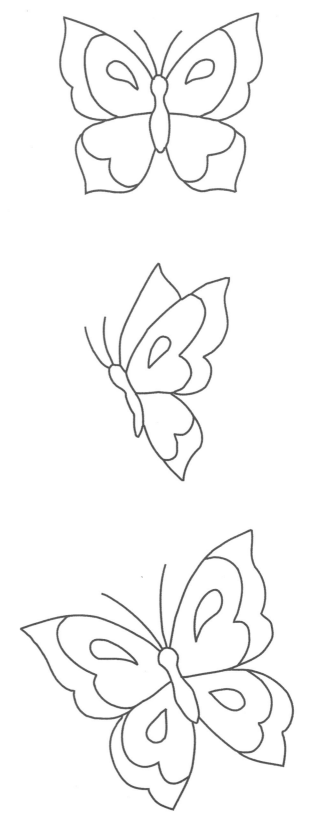

2 Apply the darker colour on top of the lighter and blend the two together to build up the colour so that the darker is towards the centre of the butterfly. When you are happy with the effect, leave to dry. Continue working around the jug until all the motifs have been completed.

3 Stand the jug upright. Touch up any gaps in the outliner. Glass paint should be touch dry in about ten minutes, but allow at least two days to harden off properly.

4 Using a clean brush, paint over the outliner with colourless varnish – this will help to protect it.

5 Repeat the same process for the tumbler, adding a single motif to one side of the glass, leaving a gap at the top for drinking.

Make tracings from these butterfly motifs to transfer the outlines on to the glassware.

Jungle Print Frames

You can almost hear the jungle drums when you see these frames –
and you don't need to go hunting for inspiration to capture the safari
spirit. To complete these simple projects, just cut out the stencils and
give it your best shot!

To get the best effect from the frame, choose a
monotone picture with a light background
colour. If you have trouble finding a suitable
picture, look in a children's annual or a wildlife
encyclopedia: use a black and white photocopy,
enlarged or reduced to fit the frame.

You will need

- Clip frame 24x18cm (9½x7in) – for the
  leopard print frame
- Clip frame 15x10cm (6x4in) – for the zebra and
  ocelot print frames
- Water-based glass paints – yellow, orange,
  brown, black, white
- Outliner paste – black
- Stencil card, film or acetate, white paper, craft
  knife, cutting mat, permanent fine marker pen
- Decorator's paintbrush – 1cm (⅜in), small
  stencil brush, soft pencil
- Typewriter carbon paper, ball-point pen
- Newspaper, kitchen paper, cotton bud,
  container of clean water, masking tape

Tracing the design

1 Trace over the animal print designs on
page 22 and 23 on to white paper with a
soft pencil. Alternatively trace directly on to
stencil film or clear acetate.

2 If you are using stencil card, cut pieces 5cm
(2in) larger than each design. Cut the
carbon paper to the same size. Lay the stencil
card on a flat surface. Over this, lay the carbon
paper, inked side facing down, with the animal
print tracing on top. Fix securely with masking
tape. Carefully go over the design lines with a
ball-point pen, pressing hard enough to ensure
a good transfer.

3 Place the stencil card, film or acetate on a
cutting mat and hold with one hand. Using
a sharp craft knife, and following the design
lines, start cutting from the centre of the
design – this will ensure the stencil structure
stays firm (see Transferring the Design,
page 8). Move the stencil around as you cut,
drawing the knife towards you.

Painting the leopard frame

1 Remove the glass from the larger clip frame
and lay it on a thick pad of newspaper.

2 Place the leopard skin stencil under the
glass, lining it up accurately with the edges
of the glass.

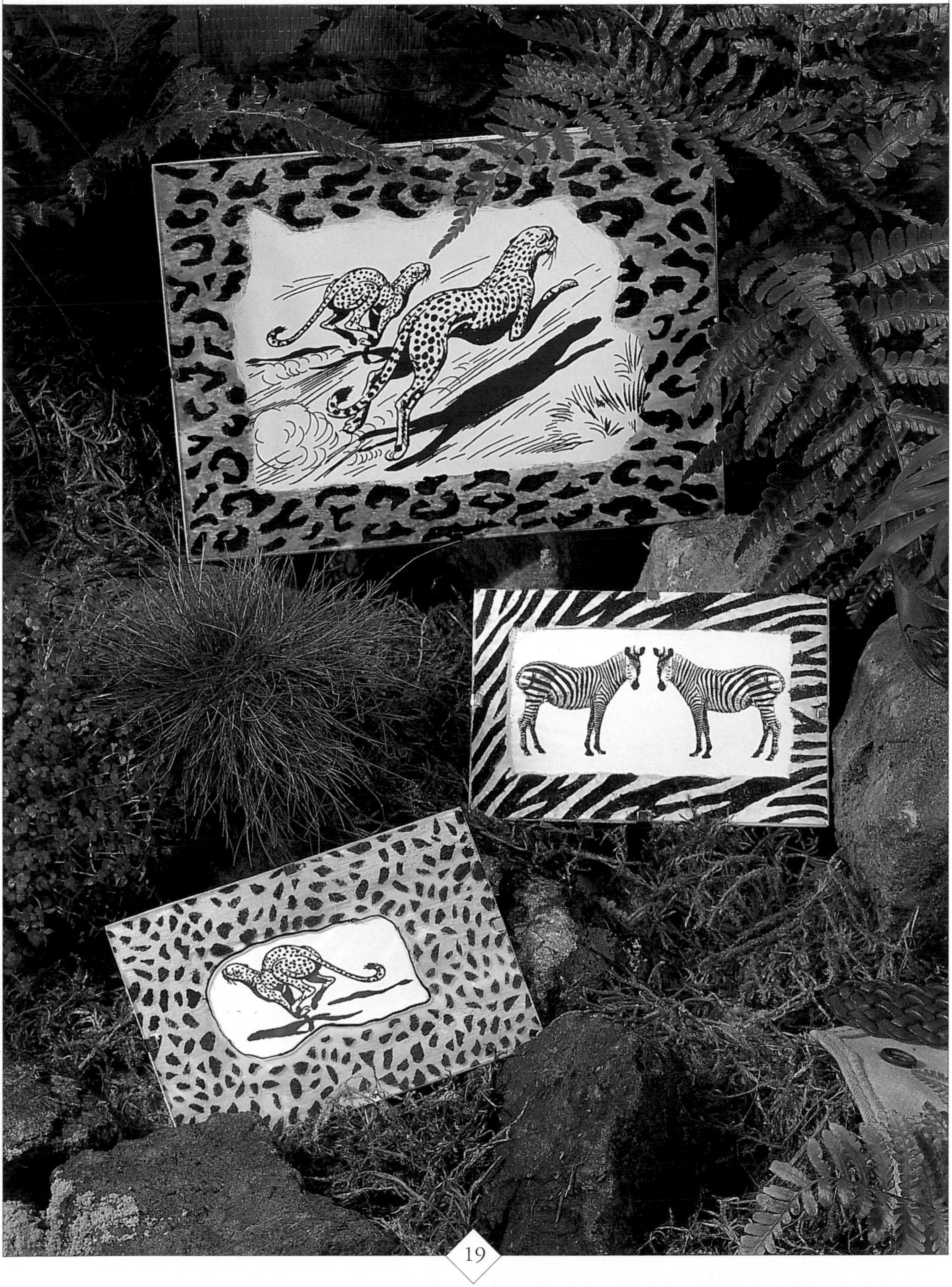

paint and the flat end of a small stencil brush, carefully pounce paint on to the surface of the glass, within the cut areas of the stencil. Leave to dry.

7 Remove the stencil from the surface, before re-assembling the frame with the painted surface on the outside.

Painting the zebra frame

1 Remove the glass from the smaller clip frame and lay it on a thick pad of newspaper.

2 Place the zebra stencil under the glass, lining it up accurately with the edges of the glass.

3 Using a 1cm (³/₈in) brush and white glass paint, cover the outer edges of the glass in the area covered by the stencil. Wipe away any paint splashes in the central glass area with kitchen paper or a cotton bud. Leave the paint to dry.

3 Using a 1cm (³/₈in) brush and yellow glass paint, make rough stripes working in one direction, around the outer edges of the glass in the area covered by the stencil. Repeat with the orange glass paint: in some areas you will see just the yellow or orange paint, in others a mottled effect caused by the paint mixing on the glass. Try to keep the paint within the border area of the design: if you do get paint on the central glass area, wipe off the excess with kitchen paper or a cotton bud. As the paint starts to dry, use a dry brush to gently merge the stripes together.

4 Using the flat end of the stencil brush, while the paint is still wet, randomly add blobs of brown glass paint to the surface.

5 Holding the brush in the palm of your hand, lightly flog the wet glass paint: this is done by tapping the painted surface with the ends of the bristles (see Paint Techniques, page 10). Flog the whole of the painted area lightly to give a furry effect to the paint while merging the paint colours together. Leave to dry overnight.

6 Remove the stencil from beneath the glass. Place over the painted top surface, in the same position as it was underneath, hold in place with masking tape. Using black glass

4 Remove the stencil from beneath the glass. Place over the painted white top surface of the glass, in the same position as it was underneath, hold in place with masking tape. Using black glass paint and a small stencil brush, carefully pounce paint on to the glass within the cut areas of the stencil. Leave to dry.

5 Remove the stencil from the surface, before re-assembling the frame with the painted surface on the outside.

Painting the ocelot

1 Remove the glass from the smaller clip frame and lay it on a thick pad of newspaper.

2 Place the ocelot stencil under the glass, lining it up accurately with the edges of the glass.

3 Draw a line using the black outliner paste just inside the area covered by the stencil. Leave to dry.

4 Using a 1cm (³⁄₈in) brush and yellow and white glass paint, make rough stripes working in one direction, around the outer edges of the glass in the area covered by the stencil. Flog the glass in the same way as the leopard design, to merge the colours and give a furry appearance. Wipe off the excess paint with kitchen paper or a cotton bud.

5 Remove the stencil from beneath the glass. Place over the painted top surface, in the same position as it was underneath, hold in place with masking tape. Using black glass paint and a small stencil brush, carefully pounce paint on to the surface of the glass, within the cut areas of the stencil. Leave to dry.

6 Remove the stencil from the surface, before re-assembling the frame with the painted surface on the outside.

Use these designs to make your own animal print
stencils.

Sunny Sunflower

Bring a touch of the Mediterranean to your home with this bright summer design. Fill the vase with home-grown sunflowers, then display with the matching plate, as a reminder of blue skies, warm seas and a land where fields of sunflowers grow

NOTE The plate should be used for decorative purposes only. The glass should be washed in warm soapy water, it is not dishwasher safe.

You will need
- Straight-sided glass vase
- Glass plate
- Water-based glass paint – orange, light yellow, medium yellow, light blue, Mediterranean blue
- Outliner paste – gold
- Water-based glass paint – colourless varnish
- Small paintbrushes, fine artist's brush
- White paper, soft pencil, masking tape
- Container of clean water
- Kitchen paper
- Scissors

Preparing the glass

1 Wash the vase and plate thoroughly in warm soapy water and leave to dry.

2 Make about twelve tracings of the sunflower: you will need less if you have a small vase. Lay white paper over the sunflower design on page 27 and draw over the outlines with a soft pencil.

3 Cut out the sunflower tracings close to the edges of the drawn lines.

4 Stick the tracings inside the vase with masking tape – have the petal tips touching where possible and use part of the sunflower tracing at the edges. Make sure each tracing is flat against the surface of the glass.

5 Using masking tape, stick a sunflower tracing to the back of the plate in the centre. Depending on the size of the plate, stick three or more part sunflowers around the edge.

Painting the outline

1 Lay the vase on its side on a pad of kitchen paper. You will be working straight on to the glass with the outliner, so it is important to practise on an old jar before you begin. The spread of the outliner depends on the temperature and humidity of the room: warm, dry conditions are best. Squeeze the tube gently

keeping your hand steady, as if using an icing tube. Always keep the kitchen roll to hand and whenever you stop, wipe the nozzle and replace the cap (see Painting Techniques, page 10).

2 Draw over the outlines of the tracings with gold outliner, working on the uppermost motifs only. Leave overnight, or as long as it takes for the outliner to dry. Turn the vase over and draw the outlines on the other side. If the vase is very large you may have to work on the vase in several smaller sections. Leave the last section to dry overnight before you start painting.

3 Place the plate flat on kitchen paper and draw over the outlines with gold outliner. Leave to dry overnight before you start painting.

Applying the paint

1 Lay the vase on its side on kitchen paper and paint the flower centres with orange glass paint (see Painting Techniques, page 10): dip the paint brush into the paint, then apply the paint to the surface of the glass, spreading it out to the edges of the outliner. Keep the thickness of the paint on the glass even,

leaving as few brush marks as you can. Work on one section at a time, leaving to dry before moving on to the next.

2 Paint the petals with the two shades of yellow glass paint, keeping the paler shade at the tips of the petals. Where the paint colours meet, use the brush to blend them together. Work on one section at a time, leaving to dry before moving on to the next.

3 To paint the background: with the vase still laying on its side, work as before on one section of the vase at a time. Paint the vase with two shades of blue paint, using a different brush to apply each colour to the surface. Use a clean brush to mix the paint together creating varying densities of colour across the surface of the vase. While still wet, use a fine artist's paintbrush or a cotton bud to draw swirls in the wet blue paint (see Painting Techniques, page 12). When dry turn the vase and complete the lower section. Paint the plate using the same technique.

4 Using a fine paintbrush, draw veins on to the sunflower petals using the darker shade of yellow.

5 Apply dots of outliner on the flower centre, concentrating the dots within the grey circle shown on the tracing. Leave to dry for about 2 days.

Sealing the surface

1 Using a fine brush, carefully paint over the outliner with colourless varnish to seal it (see Painting Techniques, page 11). Do not varnish over the glass paint or it will lose its luminosity.

2 Painted glass can be washed gently in warm, soapy water but is not dishwasher safe.

Use the sunflower below to create tracings for your vase and plate; the grey circle is a guide for painting the central dots.

All that Glitters...

At Christmas time the shops are full of expensive highly decorated baubles:
save yourself money and have fun making your own with paint, glitter and
jewels. Use bright Christmas colours as we have done; or you may prefer to
use soft shades of pink, ice blue or lilac for a less traditional look

When painting on glass baubles it is important
to remember that they are very fragile and if
you apply pressure to the surface they will
shatter. While you are painting it is advisable
to work on a tray, so that if a bauble does break
you can easily clear up the glass.

You will need

- Glass baubles, clear, frosted, shiny – white, red,
  blue, gold
- Water-based glass paint – red, blue, gold
- Outliner paste – imitation lead, silver, gold,
  bronze
- Glitter glue – red, blue, silver, gold
- Acrylic paint – gold
- Emulsion paint – white
- Glitter – silver
- Metallic embroidery thread, thick – silver
- Imitation jewellery stones
- Sequins – silver, red; gold stars
- Stiff bristled brush, soft paintbrushes, pencil
- Container of water, flat dish for mixing paint
- Kitchen paper

Working on baubles

1 When painting a bauble, hold it by the
metal hanger at the top, and work directly
on to the surface of the bauble using a
paintbrush loaded with glass, emulsion or
acrylic paint: or with a tube of glitter glue or
outliner paste. If you need to stop painting for
a colour change or just to rest your hand, use a
mug or cup as a stand to hold the bauble,
taking care that the wet paint does not get
smudged.

2 Leave the baubles to dry thoroughly
between painting with glass paint and
adding the outliner or the glitter glue. Hang
the painted baubles to dry on a make-shift line:
tie a length of string between two fixed
objects, then hang the baubles from the string
with 'S' shaped hooks made from paper clips or
fuse wire.

Using paint and glitter

1 When using outliner paste on glass baubles,
the spread of the outliner depends on the
temperature and humidity of the room: warm,
dry conditions are best. Draw the lines directly
on to the surface of the bauble with the
outliner paste, squeezing the tube gently keeping your hand steady, as if using an icing tube.
Always keep the kitchen roll to hand and
whenever you stop, wipe the nozzle and replace
the cap (see Painting Techniques, page 10).

2 When using water-based glass paint, acrylic or emulsion, apply evenly to the surface of the bauble with a soft paintbrush (see Painting Techniques, page 10). If you are worried about having an unsteady hand, draw free-hand design lines using a soft pencil on to the surface of the bauble, then fill-in with paint. Clean brushes and spills with water. Leave the paint to dry overnight. The glass paint will dry to a shiny finish, so works best when applied to a frosted bauble.

3 Glitter glue is sold in craft shops mainly at Christmas time, for decorating cards and gift wrap. Can be used directly on to the surface of the bauble like outliner paste (see Painting Techniques, page 11).

Painting the baubles

 1 On a white bauble use bronze outliner paste to make 'S' shaped lines, squiggles and dots.

 2 Paint blue glass paint over the top half of a clear bauble. When dry, make a zig-zag edge and dots using silver glitter glue.

 3 Paint gold acrylic paint on the bauble, sprinkle with silver glitter. Glue silver thread and jewels on the bauble.

 4 Using glitter glue, make alternate red and blue lines down the bauble. Glue a red sequin in the centre of each segment.

 5 Paint the surface of a clear bauble with silver glitter glue. Use lead outliner paste to draw a spiders web on the surface.

 6 Paint segments on a white bauble using white emulsion. Outline in gold outliner, then add swirls on the segments.

 7 On a red frosted bauble, paint circles using red glass paint. Glue a gold star in the centre.

 8 On a gold bauble draw 'S' shaped lines, and dots using gold glitter glue.

 9 Around the centre of a clear bauble paint a stripe using blue glass paint. Draw stars and dots using gold outliner paste.

 10 On a blue bauble paint rough star shapes using gold acrylic paint. Draw trails in gold glitter glue then attach a gold star.

 11 Use bronze outliner paste to draw small stars and dots over the surface of a white bauble.

 12 Paint lines with curly tops in red glass paint, from the bottom of a frosted red bauble.

 13 Use silver outliner paste to make squiggles on a blue bauble, sprinkle with silver glitter.

 14 Draw lines of different lengths on a gold bauble, using silver outliner paste. Sprinkle with glitter, and add silver sequins.

 15 Draw a continuous line using gold glitter glue, over the surface of a white bauble.

 16 Draw squiggles using gold outliner paste, down from the top, and up from the bottom to the middle of a blue bauble.

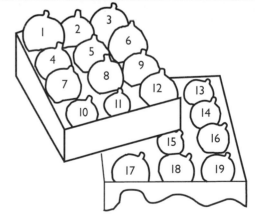

 17 On a red bauble draw 'S' shaped lines and dots using gold outliner paste.

 18 Using silver glitter glue, draw spirals on a blue bauble. Make a continuous spiral from the bottom to the top.

 19 On a red bauble, draw stars using blue glitter glue, then glue a gold star to the centre.

31

Bright Lights Supper Set

There can be no nicer way to celebrate an anniversary or birthday than with a supper party. You can make the occasion even more special by hand painting the glassware in bright cheerful colours. Use the colours and motifs we have given in the project; or choose your own to match your table linen or the occasion

Porcelain paint needs to be baked in a domestic oven to seal it on to the surface of the glass: use only ovenproof glass crockery for this project.

You will need

- Ovenproof clear glass crockery
- Porcelain paint – pink, amethyst, amber, sapphire blue
- Paintbrushes – various sizes
- Lining paper or white cloth to cover your work surface
- Soft sponge
- White spirit
- Small craft knife
- Container of clean water
- Kitchen paper

Preparing the crockery

1 Make sure that the crockery is free from grease and dirty marks: wash each item in hot, soapy water and dry thoroughly. Wipe over the surface with white spirit to remove any grease. Leave the glassware to cool before you start painting - if you work on warm glass the paint may dry too quickly.

2 When working on a cup or bowl, place it upside down, over a container like a jam jar, that will lift the glassware off the work surface. Work under a bright light and on a light-coloured surface - like lining paper or a white cloth.

3 Before starting, do bear in mind that as the glassware will be painted freehand, some brush marks will show even when the glass is baked. Also the stripes may be of varying widths, but do not worry – it will all add to the character, so long as the thickness of the paint remains the same over the entire surface of the glass.

4 Porcelain paint is water-based, so whilst painting wash your brushes regularly in water, then dry thoroughly before re-using.

Painting the striped glassware

1 For this project we have painted a bowl and a plate with the striped design, however you

may prefer to paint a different part of the dinner service.

2 Turn the bowl upside down on a container like a jam jar, then starting with the pink paint and using a soft paintbrush, make a wide stripe working from the base to the rim of the bowl. Make the journey from base to rim in one slow movement, widening the stripe as you work towards the rim. Use the brush to create a 'dragged' effect, altering the pressure of the brush on the surface and the angle of the bristles to change the width of the lines. Repeat this on the opposite side of the bowl, then find the central point between the stripes and paint two more pink stripes on each side. Leave to dry.

3 Repeat the process using amethyst paint, making a stripe on the left of each pink stripe. Leave to dry.

4 Complete the effect by painting the gaps in the design with stripes of amber paint. Any excess paint on the base can be removed with kitchen paper while it is still wet.

5 The plate is painted on the top side around the outer rim.

6 Leave the paint to dry for 24 hours, then bake in the oven, following the instructions on page 35.

Painting the spiral glassware

1 Turn the tea cup upside down on a container like a jam jar, then brush amethyst paint thickly on to the outside surface, leaving the handle and the base clear. Take a small piece of soft sponge and dab it over the wet paint to create a mottled effect. This will probably make air bubbles on the surface of the paint, continue working until the entire surface has been sponged. Leave for a few seconds then repeat the sponging process, this will remove most of the air bubbles.

2 Use the handle of a paintbrush, or a blunt object to create a spiral pattern on either side of the cup. Score the paint, so that the clear glass shows through the paint. Leave to dry.

3 Paint the handle of the tea cup with amber paint, then sponge as before.

4 The saucer is painted on the top side: brush the sides thickly with amethyst paint, leaving the base where the cup stands clear.

Sponge as before, then draw spirals in the paint: you should be able to fit eight spirals around the edge of a saucer. Leave to dry.

5 Paint the centre of the saucer with amber paint. Sponge as before.

6 Leave to dry for 24 hours then bake, see the instructions at the end of this project.

Painting the spotted glassware

1 Having positioned the bowl upside down on a container like a jam jar, paint the outside using amber paint. Make sure that the surface is evenly coated. While the paint is still wet, dab a piece of soft sponge over the entire surface the paint, creating a mottled effect. Repeat to remove the air bubbles.

2 While the paint is still wet, paint with spots of amethyst, pink and sapphire. Dab each spot with a soft sponge to soften it.

3 Leave to dry for 24 hours then bake, see the instructions at the end of this project.

Painting the flower glassware

1 Having positioned the bowl upside down on a container like a jam jar, paint the outside of the bowl with pink paint then sponge, using a light dabbing motion, to create a mottled finish. Repeat to remove the air bubbles.

2 While the paint is still wet, take the handle of a paintbrush and draw flower shapes roughly into the paint.

3 Leave the paint to dry, then gently scrape off the paint inside the flower outline using a craft knife.

4 Fill in the flowers shapes with either the amber or amethyst paint using a fine paintbrush. Sponge over each one lightly to create a mottled effect.

5 Leave to dry for 24 hours then bake, following the instructions below.

Baking the glassware

1 It is necessary to thermoharden water-based porcelain paint to make it strong enough to stand up to normal use in the kitchen, although it would be advisable not to put it in the dishwasher. Oven bake in a domestic oven for 35 minutes at gas mark 2/3, 300/325°F (150/170°C).

2 Leave to cool completely before removing from the oven.

Use these designs to mark patterns in the glass paint.

Starfish Bathroom Set

Turn your bathroom into a sea scene with this wave decorated mirror tile:
turquoise and sapphire waves splash up on to the central island of mirror glass;
while starfish swim in the foam, brought to the surface by the force of the waves –
a great way to enjoy the sea without having to leave your bathroom

You will need

- Mirror tile – 30x30cm (12x12in)
- Frosted glass tumblers
- Glass painting gel – two tubes turquoise; four tubes aquamarine; four tubes sapphire blue
- Water-based glass paint – gold
- Outliner paste – gold
- Thick plastic sheet
- Petroleum jelly, white spirit
- Blunt kitchen knife, scissors
- Masking tape, kitchen sponge
- Paintbrush, chinagraph pencil, white paper
- Hot glue gun with clear glue
- Flat dish for mixing paint, container of clean water, kitchen paper
- Cord for hanging the mirror
- Thin piece of wood 26cm (10in) long

Preparing the mirror

1 Wipe the mirror tile with a damp cloth, dry with kitchen paper, then buff with a soft cloth to remove any marks.

2 Make a tracing of the mirror centre on page 43, on to white paper using a soft pencil (see Transferring the Design, page 8). Using scissors, cut out the circular tracing.

3 Lay the tracing on to the centre of the mirror tile, then using a chinagraph pencil draw around the outer edge of the circle.

Applying the gel

1 Squeeze a line of aquamarine gel just outside the chinagraph circle on the mirror tile; add small blobs of gel just inside the line. Use the wooden end of a paintbrush or a blunt kitchen knife to create 'waves' in the gel: vary the thickness of the gel and the direction of the waves.

2 Add more aquamarine gel in a circle on top of the wet gel, again use the paintbrush or the knife to make the surface uneven, adding thickness to some of the waves (see Painting Techniques, page 11).

3 Spread the small blobs on the inside of the chinagraph line to make an uneven edge to the circle, and to cover the line.

4 Using the turquoise gel, squeeze two lines around the circle next to the aquamarine, adding a little extra towards the corners of the tile. Use the end of the paintbrush or knife to create 'waves', while merging the two colours together, creating a graduation of colour.

5 Leaving a 1cm (³/₈in) gap around the outer edge of the mirror, fill the remainder of the mirror with the sapphire gel. Use the same method as described above to create graduation of colour, texture and 'waves'. Leave to dry for several days.

Forming the mirror edges

1 Make four tracings each of the aquamarine corner and edge pieces and four of the sapphire corner and edge pieces from the outlines on pages 41 and 42.

2 Lay the corner and edge templates under the plastic sheet; you will not need to fix them, as they are only being used as a rough guide.

3 Coat the plastic sheet over the top of the templates with petroleum jelly: the jelly will stop the gel adhering to the plastic.

4 Squeeze the gel on to the plastic, over the edge and corner templates. Use aquamarine for one set of edge pieces and corners and sapphire for the other. Use the brush end or the knife to create texture and 'waves' in the gel.

5 Leave to dry for about 48 hours, but it may take longer depending on the thickness of the gel. During this time the gel may shrink.

Adding the mirror corners

1 When the strips are dry completely, gently peel them off the plastic sheet. Wipe them thoroughly with white spirit to remove all traces of the petroleum jelly.

2 Position the aquamarine corner piece on the edge of the mirror and secure in place using the hot glue gun: the corner pieces should butt-up against the gel on the mirror.

3 Using scissors, trim the aquamarine edge pieces to fit between each corner: it doesn't matter if they overlap a little. Glue in place: butting them up against the gel on the mirror.

4 Repeat using the sapphire corners and strips. To keep the strips and corner pieces

together squeeze a small amount of gel between the ends to 'glue' them together. Once this is dry add extra gel over the top to cover any rough edges, using the paintbrush end or a knife to blend the gel into place.

Making the starfish

1 Make eight tracings of the starfish on page 43, on to white paper using a soft pencil.

2 Make the starfish on the plastic sheet with the aquamarine gel, using the same

technique as for the corner and edge pieces (see Painting Techniques, page 11). When dry, remove the starfish, then wipe thoroughly with white spirit to remove all traces of the petroleum jelly. Use a spot of gel to attach the starfish to the corners of the mirror.

3 Leave the mirror to dry completely: this could take up to a week, depending on the thickness of the gel. Using a tube of gold outliner paste, draw down the points of the starfish to emphasize their shape.

Hanging the mirror

1 Take the piece of cord and tie a knot in one end. Position this approximately half way down the back of the mirror. Glue securely in place with the glue gun. Check the length of cord to ensure that it doesn't hang above the mirror and knot the other end. Trim if necessary then glue into position.

2 Cut a length of thin wood, just less than the width of the mirror and position it just above knots on the back of the mirror. Glue this in place, sandwiching the cord between it and the back of the mirror. This will give extra security to the cord.

Sponging the tumblers

1 Mask off the areas of the frosted glass tumbler that you do not want to be sponged with gold paint. Use different widths of masking tape; or use wider tape, from which you can cut narrow widths, or overlap the edges to make it wider. You can wrap the tape around the tumbler in strips; or go down the length, changing the angle slightly as you work around the tumbler.

2 Put a small amount of gold glass paint into a flat dish. Pick-up some of the paint on to a small piece of kitchen sponge, then dab onto the tumbler in the areas not covered by the masking tape. Build-up the paint with the sponge, until all the glass between the tape is covered.

3 Leave to dry overnight. Carefully peel off the masking tape, leaving gold stripes and areas of unpainted glass.

Painting the outline

1 As the tumbler is made from frosted glass, you will be working freehand straight on to the surface: using a soft pencil, copy the fish, stars, swirls and squiggly lines on page 41 on to the tumbler in the areas not covered by the sponged gold paint.

2 Lay the tumbler on its side on a pad of kitchen paper. Using gold outliner paste draw over the pencil designs (see Transferring the Design, page 9). Work on the uppermost section first, leaving time for the outliner to dry before turning the glass and moving on to the next section. The spread of the outliner depends on the temperature and humidity of the room: warm, dry conditions are best. Squeeze the tube gently keeping your hand steady, as if using an icing tube. Always keep the kitchen roll to hand and whenever you stop, wipe the nozzle and replace the cap.

3 Leave the tumbler to dry completely, then coat the painted surface of the tumbler with colourless varnish to protect it. Wash the tumblers in warm soapy water, then wipe dry.

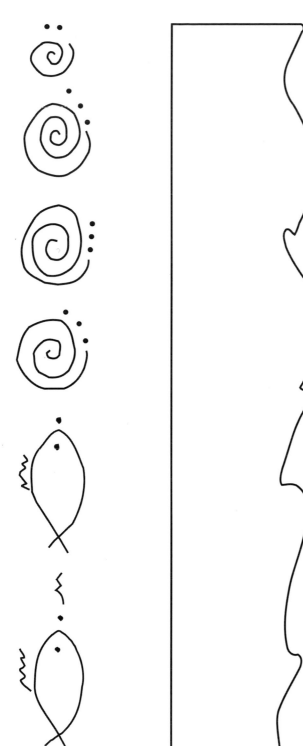

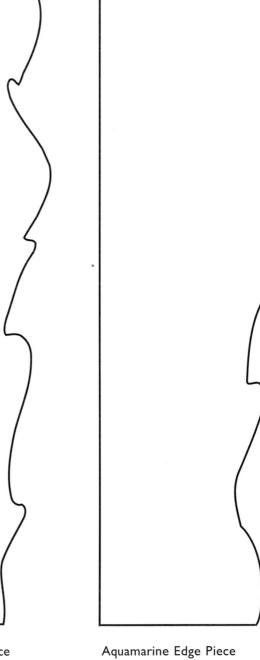

Use these swirls and fish
to draw on the tumblers.

Sapphire Edge Piece

Aquamarine Edge Piece

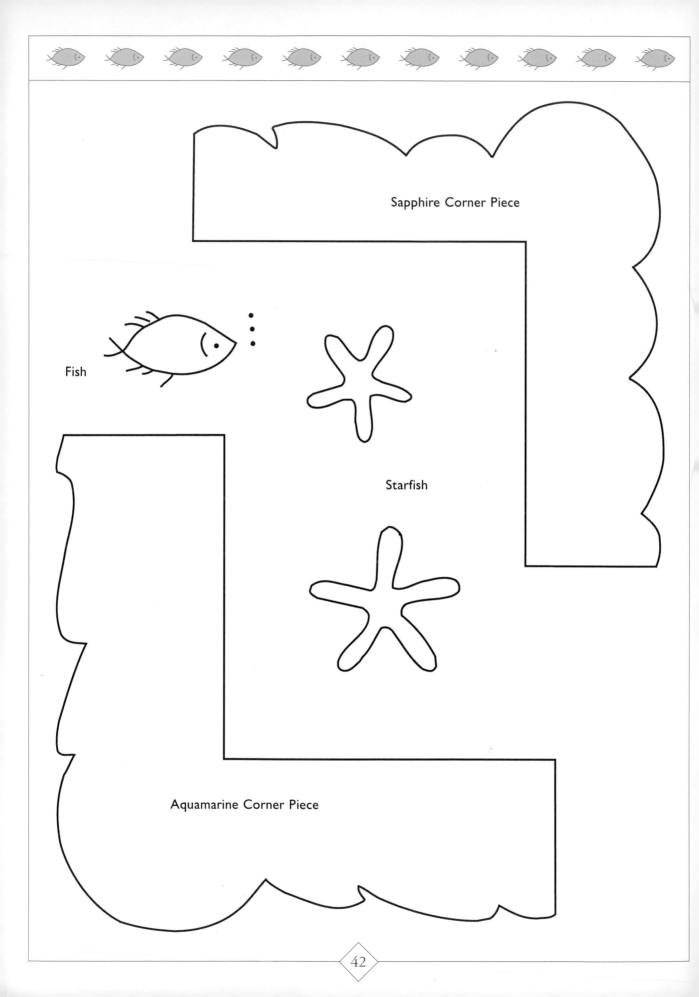

Sapphire Corner Piece

Fish

Starfish

Aquamarine Corner Piece

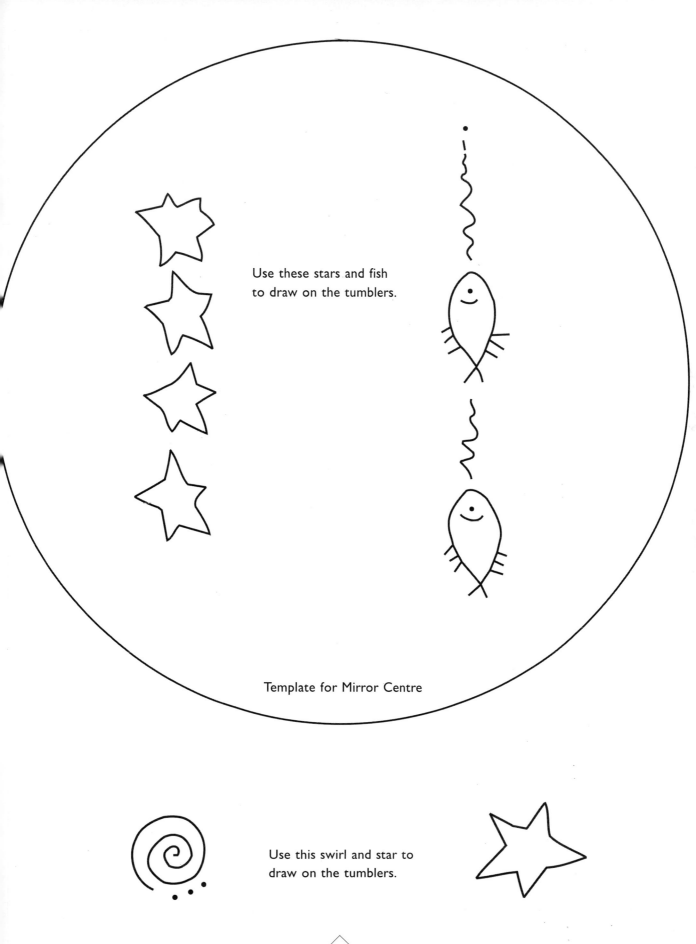

Use these stars and fish to draw on the tumblers.

Template for Mirror Centre

Use this swirl and star to draw on the tumblers.

Fruit Jam Jars

Re-cycle your old jam jars by painting them with bright fruit motifs.
Use them as storage jars in the kitchen; or give them as gifts filled with
your favourite preserve, then finish with coloured gingham tops and
hand written labels tied on with string

Decorated jam jars can be filled with preserves, but they should not be used with recipes that require the jars to be oven-heated before filling.

You will need

- Straight-sided glass jam jars
- Water-based glass paint – red, dark blue, yellow, light green, violet, pink, orange
- Water-based glass paint – colourless varnish
- Outliner paste – gold
- White paper, masking tape, tissue paper, felt-tipped pen
- Kitchen paper, cocktail stick
- Soft pencil, scissors
- Small paintbrushes
- Container of clean water

Preparing the glass

1 Wash the jam jars thoroughly to remove any grease or marks, inside and out.

2 Draw over the jar design on page 47 four times, on to white paper with a soft pencil (see Transferring the Design, page 8). Trace a different fruit into the space left on each tracing.

3 Cut the tracings so that each will fit inside a jam jar.

4 Secure a tracing inside each jar with the design facing outwards, using masking tape. You may need to hold the tracings in place with crumpled tissue, so that they stay in contact with the surface of the glass.

Painting the outline

1 Lay each jam jar on its side on a pad of kitchen paper. As you will be working straight on to the glass with the outliner, it is important to practise on an old jar before you begin. The spread of the outliner depends on the temperature and humidity of the room: warm, dry conditions are best. Squeeze the tube gently keeping your hand steady, as if using an icing tube. Always keep the kitchen roll to hand and whenever you stop, wipe the nozzle and replace the cap (see Painting Techniques, page 10).

2 Using gold outliner paste carefully draw over the design lines. Work on a small area of the design, leaving it to dry before turning the jar and completing the outlines. If you make a mistake remove the wet outliner with a cotton bud; or wait until it is dry then use a cocktail stick to gently scrape it off, adding more outliner to complete the design. Remove the design from inside the jam jar. Leave to dry overnight.

Painting the jam jars

continuing. Wash and dry the brush thoroughly in water between each change of colour.

2 Allow to harden off for about 2 days then paint over the outliner with a colourless glass paint to protect it.

Make tracings of the jar design on the next page, adding different fruits into the central space.

1 Lay each jar on its side on kitchen paper, and begin to fill in the fruit motifs with glass paint. Keep the paint even and as free from brush marks as you can, spreading the paint right out to meet the gold outlines. Use the red for the strawberries with dark blue for the background and stripes; violet for the plums with pink for the detail; yellow for the lemons with green for the detail; orange for the oranges with red for the detail. Do not work with a large area of wet paint or it may smudge or run down the face of the glass: work on small sections of the design, leaving at least 20 minutes for the paint to touch dry before

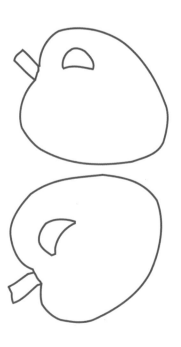

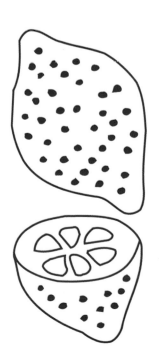

Jewelled Glass

Jewel-like shades have been combined with the Cabochon stones to create a mystical feel to this very special glassware. Send out the invitations and mix up your favourite punch; then late in the evening with friends gathered, you may just see a wizard filling the goblets with magic potion

Imitation jewellery stones have been added to the glassware in this project. They need to be glued firmly in place: it will help to protect the glue if you carefully seal the joint with outliner paste.

You will need
- Glass bowls, candle-stick, nightlight holder and goblets
- Water-based glass paint – blue, red, violet, purple
- Water-based glass paint – colourless varnish
- Outliner paste – gold
- Glass Cabochon jewellery stones
- Superglue
- Craft knife
- Small paintbrushes
- Kitchen paper

Planning the design

1 As you will be using shaped glass for this project, the outliner will need to be applied directly on to the surface of the glass without a tracing underneath. First you will need to plan the design on paper, using the shapes on page 51.

2 Following your plan, draw freehand on to the surface of the glass with outliner. If you are worried about the outliner meeting up on the other side of the glass, you can use a water soluble felt-tipped pen to draw lines on to the glass, then work over them with the outliner.

Attaching the stones

1 Using your plan for position, glue small Cabochon jewellery stones to the glass using Superglue, following the glue manufacturer's instructions very carefully. Use the stones randomly or in rows, around the sides or on the base or stem of the glassware.

Painting the outlines

1 Lay each item of glassware on its side on a pad of kitchen paper. Work on the uppermost section first, leaving time for the outliner to dry before turning the glass and moving on to the next section. You will be working straight on to the glass with the outliner, so it is important to practise on an old jar before you begin. The spread of the outliner

depends on the temperature and humidity of the room: warm, dry conditions are best. Squeeze the tube gently keeping your hand steady, as if using an icing tube. Always keep the kitchen roll to hand and whenever you stop, wipe the nozzle and replace the cap.

2 Draw a border around the rim of the glassware, adding a row of points or scallops and swirls below, similar to the designs on page 51. On the goblets draw the border towards the middle of the glass, so that the glass can be used for drinking. Leave the glassware to dry.

3 Using the gold outline paste, draw around the jewellery stones, filling in the gap between the stone and the glass (see Hints and Tips, page 13).

4 Draw irregular swirls or stars around the jewellery stones, and hearts between the stars on the uppermost section of the glass, leave to dry then continue the design on the other side of the glassware.

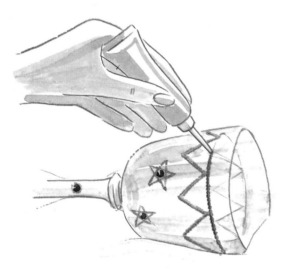

5 Using the outliner like an icing tube, apply a row of dots to the top design line of the glass.

6 After all the outlines have been drawn, leave the glassware to dry overnight.

Painting the glass

1 Lay the glassware on its side on kitchen paper and paint between the outlines using a fine paintbrush and blue, red, violet and purple paint: dip the paintbrush into the paint, then apply the paint to the surface of the glass, spreading it out to the edges of the outliner. Keep the thickness of the paint on the glass even, and leave as few brush marks as you can. Work on one section at a time, leaving to dry before moving on to the next.

2 Leave to dry then paint over the outliner with colourless paint to seal it.

3 The painted glassware can be washed gently in warm, soapy water but is not dishwasher proof.

Use these designs to create freehand borders and motifs for your glassware.

Art Deco Bottles

Inspired by the art deco period of the '20s and '30s and the designs of Clarice Cliff, these angular bottles echo the imaginative style and bold colours of that period. Recycled glass has been used with bright colours to capture the spirit of the time

Green recycled glass is manufactured in many different shapes and is readily available from homeware and gift shops. You may find that the glass contains air bubbles. These will not affect the finished design.

You will need

- Recycled glass bottle 23cm (9in) tall – green
- Recycled glass bottle 10cm (4in) tall – green
- Water-based glass paint – bright blue, bright green, violet, rose, golden yellow
- Water-based glass paint – colourless
- Outliner paste – black
- Tracing paper, felt-tipped pen, masking tape
- Typewriter carbon paper, ball-point pen, scissors
- Kitchen paper, cocktail stick, cotton bud
- Small paintbrush, container of clean water

Transferring the design

1 Wash the bottles thoroughly in warm soapy water. Leave to dry, then polish with a soft cloth.

2 Trace over the design on page 54 or page 55 with a fine felt-tipped pen. How much of the design you decide to use will depend on the size of the bottle. To establish this make a template of the bottle. Lay the bottle on tracing paper and draw around the bottle shape. Repeat for the other three sides. Cut out the four bottle side shapes.

3 Lay the bottle side shapes over the traced design, butting them together in the correct order. You may need to enlarge or reduce the design on a photocopier to fit; or you may choose to use only part of the design if you are working on a smaller bottle. Once any adjustments have been made, transfer the design to the bottle side shapes using a felt-tipped pen.

4 Cut a piece of carbon paper just larger than one side of the bottle. Attach the carbon to the bottle with tape at the top and bottom edges.

5 Lay the traced design for the correct bottle side shape on top of the carbon. Carefully go over the design lines with a ball-point pen,

pressing hard enough to ensure good transfer. Do not transfer the lines right up to the edges of the bottle. Repeat for the other sides, remove the carbon then complete the design lines around the corners of the bottle using a water-proof marker pen.

Adding the outliner

1 Paint over the carbon lines with black outliner. Squeeze the tube gently using an even pressure. Wipe the nozzle on kitchen paper frequently to stop the nozzle getting blocked. Work one side at a time, leaving each to dry before moving on to the next.

Painting the bottle

1 Lay the bottle on its side, on a pad made from a kitchen paper. Start painting each section of the design randomly, using the paint straight from the bottle on to the glass. If you are painting on green glass apply the paint more thinly than you would on clear, this helps with the luminosity of the colour. Most brush marks will disappear once the paint is completely dry.

2 Glass paint is touch dry in about ten minutes, but allow two days to harden completely. Once dry, paint over the outlines with colourless glass paint to protect it.

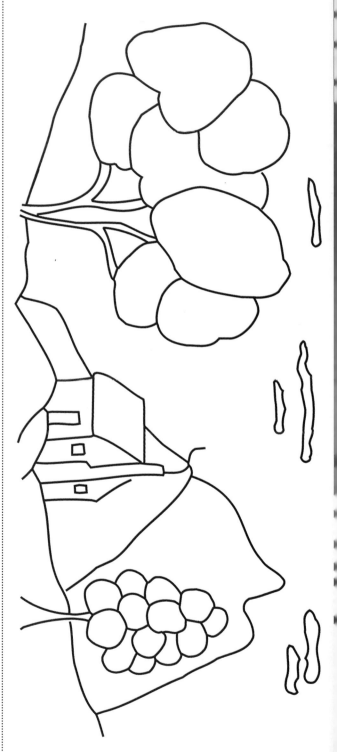

Small Art Deco Bottle

Large Art Deco Bottle

Use these designs to create your own art deco
style bottles.

Fish Mosaic

With outlines painted in lead and silver, this attractive bowl will make an unusual centre piece for your table. Spread green and turquoise glass beads over the bottom of the bowl, fill with water then add floating candles. The water will glisten with the reflections of the beads and the jewel-like fish

This project was completed using solvent-based glass paint, which has a strong smell and should only be used in a well ventilated room. If you prefer you can use water-based paint: the general working instructions are the same, but spills and brushes can be cleaned with water.

You will need

- Glass bowl
- Acetate film – A4 sheet
- Picture frame – with a 15x20cm (6x8in) aperture
- Solvent-based glass paint – turquoise, deep blue, apple green, crimson
- Outliner paste – imitation lead, silver
- Solvent-based glass paint – colourless varnish
- Glass paint thinner
- Water soluble felt-tipped pen, soft pencil, small paintbrush, scissors
- White spirit – to clean the brushes
- Double-sided tape
- Steel ruler, sharp craft knife, cutting board
- Kitchen paper, masking tape, white paper
- Flat plate for mixing paints, cocktail stick

Preparing the glass

1 Wash the bowl thoroughly in warm soapy water. When dry, polish inside and out with a soft cloth.

2 To plan the design: divide the outer surface of the bowl into four sections, then using a water soluble felt-tipped pen, draw lines from the rim of the bowl to the base, dividing the surface into four. If you have a larger bowl you may wish to add more fish.

3 Make four tracings of the fish and one bubble shown on page 61: lay white paper over the design, then draw over the outlines with a soft pencil.

4 Using small pieces of masking tape, fix one fish tracing in each section of the bowl, head to tail around the inside surface.

Painting the outline

1 Turn the bowl on to its side on a pad of folded kitchen paper. Draw over the fish outline using the imitation lead outliner paste. Squeeze the tube gently, as if using an icing tube. Work one fish at a time, leaving to dry overnight, before turning the bowl and moving on to the next.

2 Smudged or badly drawn lines can be wiped away when wet or removed with a cocktail

stick or craft knife when dry (see Hints and Tips, page 13).

Painting the bowl

1 If you are using solvent-based glass paints, make sure the room you are working in is well ventilated. When mixing colours, do not mix large quantities of paint, unless you intend to store them in screw top jars. If the paint appears too thick add a little thinner: each manufacturer uses a different solvent base for their paint, so check on the bottle to find the right thinner. Clean your brush regularly with brush cleaner or white spirit and when using paint straight from the pot use a clean brush, so not to transfer colours between pots.

2 Using a small clean paintbrush and a clean plate, mix a little green paint with turquoise to make a medium greeny-turquoise colour. Apply the paint to the top row of scales and some of the fins, working within each outlined area and right up to the outliner paste.

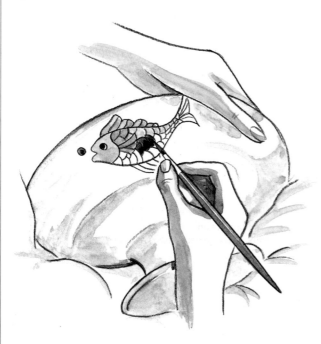

3 Solvent paints become tacky very quickly, so if the paint is too thin in one area, work quickly adding a little more paint, blending the old and new paint together with your brush. As you are using mixed paint, you may decide to work on all four fish at the same time. You can speed the drying process by using a hair dryer (see Hints and Tips, page 13), but great care should be taken not to smudge the wet paint when working.

4 For the middle row of scales, mix the paint to a violet colour using deep blue and crimson. Paint these scales taking care not to touch any areas of wet paint. To create the blue-mauve colour beneath the fin, mix turquoise paint with deep blue.

5 Fill the lower row of scales with turquoise paint, taking the colour straight from the bottle.

6 To make medium green, mix a little apple green with a little turquoise. Vary the colour by adding more apple green to make a blue-green. Apply the varying colours along the fins and tail, filling in any areas not yet painted.

7 For the head, paint apple green and turquoise straight on to the glass, blending together with the brush to give a mottled, scaly effect.

8 Fill the air bubble with a swirl of turquoise paint.

9 Stand the bowl on its base and leave to dry for at least two days.

10 Using a clean brush, paint over the outliner with colourless varnish – this will help to protect it.

11 Wash the bowl carefully in warm soapy water, and wipe dry. Polish with a soft clean cloth.

Painting the picture

1 Make a tracing of the fish design on page 61 by laying white paper over the design, then drawing over the outlines with a soft pencil.

2 Use small pieces of masking tape to attach the fish tracing to the under side of the acetate sheet.

3 On the top side, and with the acetate flat on your work surface: draw directly on to

Key for Mosaic Fish design

Medium greeny turquoise
(mix a little green paint with turquoise)

Violet
(mix deep blue paint with crimson)

Blue-mauve
(mix turquoise paint with deep blue)

Turquoise
(use straight from the bottle)

Medium green
(mix apple green with turquoise)

Blue-green
(add more apple green to medium green mix)

Greeny/turquoise
(blend apple green and turquoise on glass)

Imitation lead outliner paste

Silver outliner paste

the acetate using imitation lead outliner paste, following the design lines. Take care when using outliner on acetate for the first time. It will spread on the surface much further than it does on glass.

4 Using the silver outliner, draw over the bubbles and waves. Leave to dry.

5 Paint the fish following the instructions and colour combinations on page 58, and the diagram on page 59.

6 Fill the waves and bubbles with blue-mauve and turquoise paint. Leave to dry.

Finishing the mosaic picture

1 Using a steel ruler and sharp craft knife and working on a cutting board: cut the painted acetate to fit inside the frame. Position the picture in the frame, holding in place with double sided tape. Display the picture in a window, letting the light shine through the design, this will give an attractive stained glass effect.

Trace the whole of the design opposite to make the picture, or just the fish to decorate the bowl.

Acknowledgements

Thanks to the designers for contributing such wonderful projects:
Butterfly Jug and Tumblers (page 14), Cheryl Owen
Jungle Print Frames (page 18), Kate Fox
Sunny Sunflower (page 24), Cheryl Owen
All that Glitters (page 28), Susan and Martin Penny
Bright Lights Supper Set (page 32), Janet Bridge
Starfish Bathroom Set (page 36), Janet Bridge and Susan Penny
Fruit Jam Jars (page 44), Amanda Davidson
Jewelled Glass (page 48), Cheryl Owen
Art Deco Bottles (page 52), Lynn Strange
Fish Mosaic (page 56), Caroline Palmer

Many thanks to Ashton James and Jon Stone for their inspirational photography and
to Durand (France) for supplying the Arcopal ovenproof glassware.

Suppliers

Bostik Ltd
Ulverscoft Road
Leicester LE4 6BW
Tel: 0116 251 0015
Telephone for your local retail stockist
(Glitter glue)

Craft World (Head office only)
No 8 North Street, Guildford
Surrey
GU1 4AF
Tel: 07000 757070
Retail shops nationwide, telephone for local
store
(Craft warehouse)

Hobby Crafts (Head office only)
River Court
Southern Sector
Bournemouth International Airport
Christchurch
Dorset
BH23 6SE
Tel: 0800 272387 freephone
Retail shops nationwide, telephone for local
store
(Craft warehouse)

Home Crafts Direct
PO Box 38
Leicester
LE1 9BU
Tel: 0116 251 3139
Mail order service
(Craft equipment)

Ikea Ltd
2 Drury Way
North Circular Road
London NW10 OTH
Tel: 0181 208 5607
Retail shops nationwide, telephone for local
store
(Glassware)

Lakeland Ltd
Alexandra Buildings, Windermere
Cumbria LA23 1BQ
Tel: 01539 488100
Retail shops nationwide and mail order service
(Glass jug, tumblers, bowls, jam jars)

Squires Model & Craft Tools
The Old Corn Store
Chessels Farm, Hoe Lane
Bognor Regis
West Sussex
PO22 8NW
Tel: 01243 587009
Mail order service
(Craft tools)

Pebeo Paints (Distributor – office address only)
Philip and Tacey Ltd
North Way
Andover
Hampshire SP10 5BA
Tel: 01264 332171
Telephone for your local retail stockist
(Glass paint, porcelain paint, outliner paste,
glass painting gel)

Index